Bianca

Also by Eugenia Leigh

Blood, Sparrows and Sparrows

Bianca

Eugenia Leigh

Four Way Books
Tribeca

Library of Congress Cataloging-in-Publication Data

Names: Leigh, Eugenia, author.
Title: Bianca / Eugenia Leigh.
Description: New York : Four Way Books, [2023]
Identifiers: LCCN 2022033079 (print) | LCCN 2022033080 (ebook) |
ISBN 9781954245440 (paperback) | ISBN 9781954245457 (epub) |
Subjects: LCGFT: Poetry.
Classification: LCC PS3612.E35655 B53 2023 (print) | LCC PS3612.E35655
(ebook) | DDC 811/.6--dc23/eng/20220712
LC record available at https://lccn.loc.gov/2022033079
LC ebook record available at https://lccn.loc.gov/2022033080

This book is manufactured in the United States of America and printed on
acid-free paper.

Four Way Books is a not-for-profit literary press. We are grateful for the assistance
we receive from individual donors, public arts agencies, and private foundations
including the NEA, NEA Cares, the Literary Arts Emergency Fund, and the
New York State Council on the Arts, a state agency.

We are a proud member of the Community of Literary Magazines and Presses.

Contents

Notes

I.

Do I not look in the mirror,
these days,
and see a drunken rat avert her eyes?
Do I not feel the hunger so acutely
that I would rather die than look
into its face?
I kneel once more,
in case mercy should come
in the nick of time.

— Anne Sexton

What I Miss Most about Hell

is prayer.
I'd pack a plastic bottle

with vodka, drive
to the crag of my life—

the parking lot of a pancake house—
and scream. I prayed

like everyone I loved was on fire.
The bright, violet blob

I called God
would forgive the atrocities

roared in ethanol
while I'd shake like a dog

demanding answers
from the maker of figs:

why the sycamore fruit
sweetens only when bruised,

the way a fist will
ripen a child.

The First Leaf

I thought I forgave you. Then I took root and became
someone's mother. This unending dread, ever checking

for his breath. I have never wanted to be less like you
than I do now, daily gauging the venom,

how much of you blights my blood. When my baby wails, I ask
whether I too could beat his body quiet. And when I choose

to be a mother, choose to be tender to my child—a choice
my mangled brain makes each day—my fury surges.

The distance between him alive and him dead
is how well I am. And I think about the woman in the news

who poured water on her sleeping baby's face. And I
think how for decades, I was grateful you never killed me. How

that was enough to make me think you loved me.
I raged as a child, but never

in the right direction. So when my therapist said
that not killing me yet didn't mean not killing me ever—

that if I had stayed, I would have died—I had to
watch her get angry to know to get angry.

On the eighth week of the pandemic, my son, whom I sheltered
at home for all that time, found on our fifth-floor balcony

a tiny green leaf the width of his pinky.
The last time we'd strolled outside, the city was frigid. Frost

everywhere we looked. And Dad, let me tell you, the leaf
stunned us both. Unexpected, like the olive branch

snatched by the dove barreling back to the ark.
He refused to let go—the first leaf of all the leaves

my child will ever hold. He looks so much like his father.
Nothing at all like us.

Family Medical History

The heart doctor glues
tubes to my torso to monitor
the million warring citizens within me.

The machine belted to my body says
the battle has simmered
to a discussion:

my heart in constant murmur.
Not harmful, just loud.
I believe

a man who'd chase his baby with a knife
makes up half my blood.
I believe his demons

sleep in volcanoes bobbing in my veins.
The gut doctor slides a scope
down my esophagus and prescribes

a pill packed with moons
to expose all that crawls
in my unlit caves.

And I am thinking of the story
of the pregnant dog, maimed
by a crash. How her pups learned

to walk with their hind legs
dragged, parroting
their mother's injury. How we mimic

the dysfunction modeled for us.
The bone doctor points to a diagram
of legs to explain the ache

in my knees. The brain doctor suggests
I forgive myself.
You were not the abuser, she says.

You are the child.

Undiagnosed

When my father kidnapped us,
I didn't want to go home. I wanted to be

feral. I wanted to test my luck.
Plane rides fall short of that first plane ride,

bookended by police. Men fail
to meet his standard of surprise. Three a.m. wakings

on school nights. Sometimes to whip us
for imagined sins, sometimes

to dance. I need to see the music
quaking in the furniture. Chair legs jittering, cheap wood

threatening to split. I took my first steps outside this country
with a herd of church kids

on my nineteenth birthday. I convinced them to drive
to Tijuana. That's how I found the one

I bribed to drag the virgin out of me.
Before I tried to kill him, I saw ten nameless angels

bungling about his dorm. Then
the torment set in. I wouldn't leave my top bunk for weeks.

We never saw my father sleep
when it was time to sleep. He wound around the house at night,

a broken or horrifying toy that wouldn't shut off.
Or he slept for weeks.

I was the one who would risk
rousing him to check. Thirty years

I lived with the urge to run into traffic. And did.
Windows thrown open, floor-standing

rosewood speakers flooding our home with rock operas,
we couldn't hear our voices.

That's when we knew he was happy.
That's when we knew we could breathe.

Post-Traumatic Stress Disorder with Secret Knock

My hand, soaked in blood.
My head, cracked open. I tell

the five-year-old to fetch the phone.
The two-year-old to fetch a towel.

My hand, soaked in blood,
holds the towel to my head,

cracked open. The children—
their round eyes, black planets

smacked off their orbits.
And the hostess

to whom I say, *May I please
speak to Jennifer*, our mother,

who has left us alone
again. And the number, a number

we practiced. *For exactly this,* I think,
proud. And I, the oldest,

age six, calm, calmer
than I am now, a mother

who, alone with my baby, kills
the lights, hides in the bathroom

because someone is at the door,
and we must never answer the door.

And I scream at my spouse
because why the fuck are flowers

arriving when I am home alone
because I forget who I am or how old.

And the chair we keep by the door
for climbing, for bolting

the chain. And the wait, the length
of her shift, for the secret knock,

a knock (I now know)
everyone knows. And the diagnosis:

retraumatized. And the infant,
lifted from my womb split open.

And the stitches on my gut.
And the stitches on my head.

And the blood on my hand
holding my child brain bits in.

And the blood on the pads I filch
from the hospital. And the hospital

where our mother tells the doctor
a lie to keep them

from taking us away. And the hospital
where, between contractions,

they ask whether I feel safe
at home, safe enough

to take the baby back with me.
And by instinct, I say yes,

but for a second, I am tripped again,
six again, and I am lying.

Prayer with Strawberry Gelatin

My sister is sick.
The culprit—shapeless, anonymous.

Medical science works best with a villain:
name the devil

to learn whether to cut loose a tumor, switch out
a liver, break into heart after heart.

Will it help her to know
she dodged a knife

in the womb? Has she already heard?
In the memory of that day,

I ask
whether the hospital feeds our mother Jell-O.

Mom is alive.
I am four. I associate strawberry gelatin with miracles,

and the baby is okay.
Once, in Galilee, spit and a pair of hands

gave sight to a blind man,

but not on the first try.   My sister's storm

needs a name, Lord. She points to her temples

where her torrents are born.

Bipolar II Disorder: First Evaluation

Someone in a gunmetal trench coat stares— across the street—
on Fourteenth— light flips green— he stays put—

I stalk by— nod— he nods back— I veer right, stride south— the itch
to swing around— if he's still there, human— if not, angel—

I glance back— gone— nowhere in sight— a sighting,
I'm sure— so sure, so sure, I float home— *high episodes of euphoria—*

someone's wedding lopsided on a hill— can't keep still—
distractibility— drink till I can't drive— then drive

to five years ago— fuck in his new bed— can't sleep— never sleep—
decreased need for sleep— gun it at dawn— to what wrecked

five years ago— fuck this one on the floor— *excessive
involvement in pleasurable activities— with high potential for painful consequences—*

let's call them painful consequences— the one who strapped me
to his motorcycle— the one who trapped me in his shower— the one

whose sister tried to die— who couldn't unless he choked me—
who could, but on the rooftop— in the conference room—

at the bar— *sexual indiscretions*— or, years prior,
down twelve acetaminophens— twin dorm bed— bed,

always in bed— *hopelessness*— *major depressive episodes*— then—
 mid-try— a bright pull to rise— why die when I can swim to Paris—

Manhattan— you can't swing a dead cat without snagging a poet
in Manhattan— *flight of ideas*— *inflated self-esteem or grandiosity*—

and can't I shut up— all caps— and turn down the music— cranked
high— blaze down Pacific Coast Highway past midnight— past midnight,

break into the Hollywood Bowl to dance— scale the stage— then
dance— decide to learn— decide to learn to dive— to silk—

to climb— a new language— *I need help* in seven thousand languages—
increase in goal-directed activity— and the poet in me, a sucker

for endings— seven thousand ways to end— none of them lush enough—

June Fourteenth

My children, if I may call them that,
that identical pair of beans, quick to arrive

then quick to die, quit my body
a year ago today. Not quit—I opted

for the D&C to say: they didn't leave,
I did nothing to make them leave,

they were taken in my sleep.
The animal I became

conjured the animal I once was.
Fiend and brute and wretch. Back

to the wreck my husband had never met.
And that lie, hounding

since the first night I woke howling
next to him, startled, tentative:

this life doesn't belong to you. I was warned
about the nightmares. That in our first years

of marriage, my hells
would hunt me in my sleep.

All my life, my mother locked
our knife block beneath the kitchen sink.

Did you know not all women hide
their knives from their husbands?

I married a man who owns a knife sharpener.
He slices everything soundlessly,

the way he learned in a class about knives.
I chop our produce with an air

of panic, like a child
who found the murder weapon.

My husband once leapt out of a closet
in the dark. To make me laugh.

I wept. No one prepares you for the terrors
of a good man.

lograr las ilusiones. Eso me motivó a estudiar psicología experimental en la universidad.

Traer revistas de comercio a la biblioteca

Las revistas científicas, de comercio y periódicos de negocios pueden enseñar a los estudiantes una amplia variedad de carreras y ayudar a que estos estudiantes tengan oportunidades a su disposición después de graduarse. Cada profesión, desde la más compleja a la más práctica, cuenta con su propio periódico. Estos se publican sobre campos tan diversos como banca, panadería, funcionamiento de lavado de coches, construcción, mantenimiento de edificios, electrónica y muchos otros. Los padres que ya trabajan en estos campos podrían traer sus viejos periódicos de negocio a la biblioteca de la escuela. Estas revistas serían una ventana al mundo del trabajo y ayudaría a motivar a los estudiantes.

CAPÍTULO 2: ENSEÑANZA Y EDUCACIÓN

Mientras los estudiantes están en la escuela elemental, los profesores pueden involucrarles fácilmente utilizando un interés especial para motivar su aprendizaje. Un ejemplo consistiría en coger el interés de un estudiante por los trenes y usar un tema sobre trenes en muchas asignaturas distintas. En clase de historia, leer sobre la historia del ferrocarril; en clase de matemáticas, poner trenes para resolver un problema; en clase de ciencias, discutir las distintas formas de energía que utilizan los trenes anteriormente y en la actualidad, etc.

Cuando los estudiantes asisten a la escuela secundaria y a la superior, pueden emocionarse visitando lugares de trabajo interesantes, como una construcción, una empresa de arquitectura o un laboratorio de investigación. Esto proporciona una idea real de una carrera para el estudiante, quien empieza a comprender el camino educativo que debe tomar desde temprano en la escuela hasta conseguir esa carrera. Si no es posible visitar un lugar de trabajo, invita a padres que tengan trabajos interesantes a la clase para hablar con los estudiantes acerca de su trabajo. Se recomienda encarecidamente que lleven muchas imágenes para mostrar la realidad física de ese trabajo. También es una oportunidad para los estudiantes poder oír acerca del lado social del trabajo, lo que puede proporcionar motivación para hacer nuevos amigos, unirse a grupos o aventurarse en situaciones sociales que al principio podrían parecer desagradables.

Los estudiantes en el espectro necesitan estar expuestos a cosas nuevas para interesarse en ellas. Necesitan ver ejemplos concretos de cosas realmente divertidas para que los mantenga motivados para aprender. Yo quedé fascinada por ilusiones ópticas después de ver una sola película en la clase de ciencias. Mi profesor de ciencias me retó a recrear dos famosas ilusiones ópticas, llamadas la Ames Distorted Room y la Ames Trapezoidal Window. Pasé seis meses haciéndolas en cartón y madera contrachapada. Finalmente conseguí

My mother still calls
to ask whether our doors are locked.

Maybe there is no cure for this. The way
the brain bends after trauma

and bends the world with it.
Even now, a baby cross-legged inside me,

I scan the day for traces of soot
sullying this honeyed life. Who was it,

years ago, who told me—
afraid and wracked with undeserving—

to find a mirror
and look myself in the eyes?

Children of Lions

The rest of us,
trembling among our mothers'

bargain trench coats, waited
for Narnia. There, we dreamed

we were the children
of lions. Heirs to our own beds. Safe

in a closet rapturous with centaurs
in symphony with naiads and fauns. And I,

pink and young, swelled like a sinless sun. And I
pretended my father—

who had struck me then shoved me in—
would find my tomb empty

and repent. No, that is the adult talking.
I was a child then. It didn't matter

what he'd done.
I still wanted to be found.

Post-Traumatic Stress Disorder with Rovelli's Theories of Time

A crude green shoot
astonished to wake in a glacier,

my second attempt
sprouted out of nowhere.

I was happy then. How
did the pills find my throat?

The entire universe is like a mountain
that collapses

in slow motion. My brain, snared
sometime before I could speak

and after my last benzo,
endures a mode of time

truer than the ticking. *The passage*
from one moment of time to the next

is illusory. Was I
the woman or the child

when on the phone with my father
who phoned often to say

he planned to kill himself?
Again and again he said this

for hours as I lay in the lap
of a man who, just a boy, supplied

the joints that singed my lips.
What came first?

The calls or the pills? The Bible says
God made the sun

days *after* he made light,
days *after* he made days.

Why bother with a sun at all?
That fiction of seasons, of healing

time swears it'll fetch
but fails to bring. My father's fists,

that boy in the fog, those years
I, tanked out of my wits,

baited bruisers at bars
because I couldn't take how I could

feel the blows, can feel them now,
but found no marks

on my body—a discrepancy
I needed to machete from my brain.

When I was pregnant
and petrified

of giving birth to my father,
I found him in a dream,

bloodied and writhing,
bound by chains in my shower.

Yes, I found my father
bound in the one place where,

during the worst of it,
I'd bare my fears and pray.

I Was Wrong about So Much

About my brain, its wires glitching
like a jellyfish sprite

flashing its apple-red tentacles
above my countless thunderclouds.

About your eyes, not a savior's eyes
but brown as blood. I was wrong

about the God I warped
into a weapon, a garrison.

Wrong about love, too. I thought love
was my mother's soprano tessitura

screaming. I thought love was
a violence. Verdi's requiem, *Dies irae*.

You thought love
was love. New millennium emo. February

flooding the school below the palms
wringing their palms

like willows the morning after
you rinsed gas station zin from my hair.

I'm sorry I chased you for years
the way a cowbird tails the cow—

not for love of the beast,
but for the insects it kicks up.

She ditches her eggs
in someone else's nests

to do this. Kills someone else's young
to do this. *This* possessed. I was.

My Father Erupts

from a seven-year estrangement
to die, for good this time,
of a flood
sloshing around his lungs
as cancer climbs up his neck.
I wanted better
reunion music. I wanted him
to go out singing.

The best word I've got
is *noisy.* His dying, noisy. And this
in the year of apocalypses. The fires,
the virus, the human
rights abuses a blur against
the din of his vituperative exit.

Elegy Composed in the New York Botanical Garden

Catmint—tubular, lavender, an ointment
to blur the scar, bloom the skin. My mouth has begun
the hunt for words that heal.

In the garden, I am startled by a cluster
of sun-colored petals marked, *Radiation.*
Piles of radiation. Orange radiation, huddled together

like families bound by a hospital-bright morning.
And behind them: a force of yuccas
called *Golden Swords.* A bush or mound

of sheath-like leaves sprouting from a proud center.
And isn't that the plot?
First the radiation, then the golden sword.

I remember, incurably, your mother. The laughter
that flowered from her lips. I'm sorry
I have no good words to honor her war.

Consider the Sun

The winter God failed to jolt her young liver to life,
I wandered through a home of broken mill spokes.

Below the attic's exposed insulation
leaned a stack of unhinged doors—the first

marked *Have you found what you're looking for*,
a handwritten *No* below it—and beyond the doors

wobbled a lone dresser drawer holding a flask
and a book from 1948 called *Come Be My Love*.

Past a tapestry rolled to the ceiling slats,
I found a bare room where children must have spilled

lagers and swapped *Playboys* next to the shelf
laced with webs. And in the corner of that room,

look: the jagged skull of a dead thing
who once swung its antlers at a live thing.

Imagine them both, wanting to live. Another chance
to consider the sun, put food to mouth.

Is it better to die in the struggle or to survive it,
then die decades later alone with a cognac, a book,

and no fight left in your bones?

Matrescence

The fire in the news sets loose
the bulwarks in my brain. They protect me
by compiling all the ways to die.

I am not the kind of woman who prays
to be spared from the fire.
The fires will come, I know. But I can't help

asking my midnight questions,
rotten questions sour in the mouth.
How to be mother enough,

how to save my child
when the blaze comes for us.
What I know of mothering is this:

my mother often locked herself in a room
to pray for hours until she couldn't
see out of her swollen, scarlet eyes.

Spare us from the fire, spare us from the fire,
she'd wail as we knocked.
Spare us from the fire, spare us

from the fire, she'd wail
even as she packed us up
to move back in with it again and again

each time the fire showed up
to beg on its knees
even after we painted our red car blue

so we couldn't be found.
When I fear I am
the kind of mother my mother was,

I have to keep in mind
the end: she did eventually take the three of us
and flee. The marks on her body

took ten years to fade.
And still, on my right arm, the faint stain
of a burn. I've been trained by now

to outrun the devil
and outcock the pocket-sized devils he lobs
from a distance. But remind me—

in the legend, who stood
in the king's furnace with the three
who walked out of the flames
unbound, unharmed, not a stick of hair singed?

Glossolalia

My baby brandishes a wooden knife
meant to halve a wooden shallot

as he hollers his newest word. *Knife.*
Look at my son, flashing

his dagger, jamming it into plush
animals. *Knife, knife.* Look at him,

oblivious to the weapons
littering his lineage or, God forbid,

possessed by them. Can the babies
planted in the dirt of our bodies

absorb the torments buried there?
My gentle, watchful child

wants all the knives. But some days,
everywhere, *blue.* The bear, *blue.*

The bells, *blue,* the car, the cup,
the light. I marvel at my son,

who marvels at the sky—*blue, blue*—
no matter how gray the bully of clouds.

And this is all I want.
Look at my son laughing at the rain.

Look how he prods the window
with his knife, insisting

we cut up the storm, demanding
the blue back into view.

On Spiritual Bypassing

It's true, the girl I envied most growing up
scorched her hand because she grazed an angel
perched on her Bible. I lusted after

her pluck, her gutsy resolve to burn herself
over and over as angel after angel seemed to show up
for the sheer sport of it. We belonged to a people

who lined up to be thrown several pews
back by an anointed tap on the head,
which is to say, they all believed her, and I did, too,

raised by a zealot who could tally
the angels and demons in a room, then howl
until only the seraphs remained.

But see how now the fire blows out
when I ask about my sister. The divided crowds
multiplying in her mind. Our mother's eyes

fogged over. They eschew the doctors, insist I pray,
and another rock drops into my pocket
while I dream about the time I tried to walk

across a lake. Despite all that was written
about the charismata, their mysterious distributions,
I was prodded constantly to open my mouth

and moan for the Spirit with my spirit.
But it was wisdom I wished for—
the kind that threatens to halve babies

to save them. It was always the baby
I wanted to save. When her havoc continued,
I blamed myself. It wasn't easy

unlearning how to beg for help this way.

This City

could use more seraphs.
Anything with wings, really—

a falcon, a caladrius.
Ravenous for marvels, I slit open
a chrysalis. Inside,
no caterpillar mid-morph.
Only its ghost in a horror of cells.
I pinch the luminous mash
of imaginal discs
and shudder, imagining
the mechanics of disintegration.
The wormy larva—whole,
then whorled. A wonder
it did not die. Even now,
smeared against my skin, it beams

like the angel in the tomb
prepared to proclaim a rising.

II.

The flowers bloom even when I barely water them.
Some flowers sprout even though the soil is parched.
Those kinds of flowers are terrifying.

— Kim Yideum

The Part of Stories One Never Quite Believes

It's not the story though, not the friend
leaning toward you, saying "And then I realized—,"
which is the part of stories one never quite believes.
I had the idea that the world's so full of pain
it must sometimes make a kind of singing.

— Robert Hass, "Faint Music"

The year I hid in a convent, I met zero nuns. Instead, I met a group of young AmeriCorps service members who earned their convent beds in Boyle Heights, Los Angeles by drilling subtraction into underprivileged kids or scrubbing showers for unhoused people on Skid Row.

I don't know how my friend Shannon convinced her convent-mates to take me in, but they gladly dragged an extra mattress into a spare room, and when their stipends hit their bank accounts, they readily shared their beer.

It was the same year a tattoo artist in San Jose refused to ink the back of my neck because he said I would regret it. I'd spent the entire morning with a protractor making up a symbol that had no meaning. He didn't budge even when I returned the next day.

I remember that year in flashes. It began around 6 a.m. on a December Monday in Seoul, when I lied to my father. I hugged him. Told him I was off to my first day of work at a tutoring center that actually existed and had offered me an actual job.

But instead of walking to work, I ducked into a subway station, crashed down a set of stairs, tumbled—broken bag, torn slacks—into a train full of horrified commuters, and wound up at Incheon International Airport to fly six thousand miles away.

I don't remember what convinced me I was better off jetting without warning than having a reasonable conversation with my father. I believed I was in danger. Whether that was fact or paranoia is hard to say. I do recall that all I'd stuffed into the laptop bag, in addition to the laptop I stole from my father, was underwear.

I've played and replayed that morning in my mind. Shoving, then unshoving my getaway items into and out of the laptop bag. Deciding, finally, that my most pulsing concern was the possible embarrassment of my father finding lace thongs among my abandoned belongings.

And my one inconsequential yet enduring regret: not taking the royal blue coat he'd bought me during my first week in Seoul. *Why don't you wear your new coat to work?* he'd asked when I woke him.

I said it wasn't cold enough. Or maybe that it was too cold. I loved that coat with a devotion objects don't tend to elicit from me. That much-too-expensive, much-too-adult coat outshining the rest of my thrift store wardrobe and purchased by a man who patched a dozen odd jobs together to make a living for himself. I thought maybe he would sell it when I was gone. I hadn't anticipated him destroying it with the rest of my things.

I had planned to live with my father for a year after college. Perhaps to make up for the decade he was either in prison or, post-deportation, in a country I'd never known. But this was before I understood the mechanics of memory. How it's possible to rewrite a father as someone less like a violent and convicted felon and more like a wounded soldier.

I also didn't understand what prison does to a person—especially a person with unaddressed mental illnesses. Why anyone would want to live in a studio with every window blocked with boxes. It shouldn't have surprised me that I was allowed only certain amounts of food and only occasional phone calls, but it did.

The more I observed my father's erratic habits, the faster homesickness devolved into a kind of terror. I had flashbacks of beatings, of my mother's 911 calls. Then, rattled by nightmares of my childhood plus my father's pleas that I stay for two, maybe three, years, I started to make hysterical and secret phone calls. Enlisted an army of humans back in California willing to help me escape.

What kind of daughter flees in panic from her father—days before their first Christmas in years—on a morning he gives her a hug, tells her he is proud of her, and insists she have a good day at work? The kind who doesn't deserve Christmas. I boycotted the holidays that month.

I hadn't yet gone to see my mother or sisters since I'd landed at LAX. The guilt of betraying my father, who emailed daily bulletins of anguish and anger, spiraled into a narrative that convinced me I should be sentenced to a life without family, too.

So I made a nest for myself on a friend's futon while wasting most of my days sucking on a liter of cheap tequila and crafting a mixed CD with songs about black hearts and self-harm for another friend who'd convinced me to meet him in the parking lot of a desolate mall on Christmas Day. He was concerned. They all were. But their kindness only fueled the unrelenting voice telling me I didn't merit their care.

I've heard plenty about our deserving to be loved. But what do we deserve when we might have squandered our love stash? I became the kind of woman who cheated on a man who got caught in the crossfire of my self-loathing. Then eventually, the kind of woman who slept with men I found revolting simply to prove I didn't care what happened to my body.

During that year, I returned to bartending six nights a week at a Los Angeles karaoke bar I'd worked for in college. That following November, I volunteered to bartend on Thanksgiving mostly because it felt redundant to boycott the holidays for two years in a row.

The scheduled karaoke jockey, bitter because he did not volunteer to work, hosted an early turkey dinner for us self-proclaimed orphans—a crew of mostly bar colleagues and our dearest alcoholic friends. It would be a slow night. The owners wouldn't be there. We all drank. We all drove. We all lilted happily into work.

I can conjure the rest of what I remember in spurts cut with static. I remember two frat-boy types entered the empty bar. They took the stools closest to the server station and asked for Jägermeister shots. It was the cocktail waitress who suggested a round of shots for all of us. Then another.

I burned my arm on the exposed cash register light reaching for a bottle of Hennessy, which I took a shot of, too. Chester, my favorite regular, eyed me warily as he ate the Thanksgiving leftovers we brought him. I grew wild and manic and all the best and worst kinds of loud.

It was the year I had a drinking problem, which I waved away as "a life problem." It was the year my bipolar disorder burgeoned, which I blamed on birth control pills. I was young and unconquerable. I drove drunk because I wanted to die, but by God's grace, the worst thing I ever did was shear off the side view mirrors of an entire block of parked cars.

And maybe that's the ticket: grace. It was the year I expected harsh karma, but instead, I called my friends from the gutters of Hollywood, and they picked me up. Every time. Even when I cursed at and punched them as they folded me into their cars.

I roamed the streets wasted in miniskirts. Once, a golf cart—van?—full of men in blurry uniforms—cops?—drove me to an alleyway and parked next to a dumpster. They got out a first aid kit and patched up my bloody knees. They waited with me until I sobered up enough to call someone to pick me up and take me home. And no, they didn't rape me.

I remember my hands grabbing every emptied bottle of liquor from what turned out to be a busy Thanksgiving night and shaking them dry into a single, plastic cup. I remember downing that cup: a trash can shot.

Then after two hours of utter nothingness, during which I'm told the server cleaned up the bar for me and closed out my cash register, I remember screaming at the bouncer and calling him a thief. I accused him of stealing my tips and of worse offenses as he laughed and apologized to the taxi driver he'd phoned to drive me home.

My first memory of the taxi ride is puking in the backseat. Having moved almost every year of my life and having recently found an apartment in Pasadena after months of hopping from couch to convent, I had no idea where I lived. That's my next memory: shouting cities and numbers to cobble together an address that might mean home.

After some magic or trickery, when the taxi driver arrived in front of the place to which I had a key, he opened the back door of the cab, and I fell out bawling. I had no money to give him except a rotten pile of singles. He refused my cash. I shouted, though I didn't mean to shout. I told him I would pay to clean his car. I begged him to come back to the bar to find me.

I woke up the following morning on the floor of the living room I shared with Craigslist strangers. I needed a ride to go back to work that evening, so I phoned Shannon, who, two years later, would become the friend who would send carnations in a margarita glass to commemorate the last time I served a drink from behind a bar. She'd graduated from the convent life and now worked at a hospital.

Shannon picked me up in the early afternoon on her way to her hospital shift. A crucifix dangled from her rearview mirror, and the stickers on her back bumper declared feminist exhortations such as "Well-behaved women seldom make history."

I remember Shannon spoke, and while I don't remember the words she used, I recall the heat of her tone. I adjusted my fishnets and said nothing. It was the year I couldn't parse the difference between care and condemnation. Whatever she said made me feel judged and angry. Hateful even. Conjuring it now, over a decade later, I see that, too, was love.

Because I was afraid to show my face at the bar until the absolute last minute I had to be there, I sat alone at the McDonald's next door with a Filet-o-Fish. I sat on that unforgiving red bench for three hours on the Friday after Thanksgiving. A secular confessional. Then when I felt inside my purse for my phone to check whether it was time to finish my sentence at McDonald's, I found this handwritten note:

MY NAME IS EDWARD, I WAS WORKING AS A TAXI
THANKSGIVING EVE. I GOT A CALL TO THE BRASS MONKEY
& BROUGHT YOU HOME. YOU PUKED IN MY BACK SEAT,
& OVER THE MOST OF ME. I CANNOT QUITE UNDERSTAND
WHY THERE WAS NO ONE TO CARE FOR YOU
ESPECIALLY ON A NIGHT LIKE THIS. IF YOU WISH TO CALL ME
YOU MAY. (818) XXX-XXXX CELL

I surrendered. I wept and wept under those obscene fluorescent lights as I thought about the taxi driver. The AmeriCorps workers. The friend who stood in the cold with me on Christmas. I thought about the tattoo artist.

The friends at the bar. Shannon. I'd tried so damningly hard to punish myself and cut myself off from family, yet it felt as though some higher author had invaded my story with a cast of characters all fighting for the role of the Good Samaritan.

It was the year I most hated myself, but also the year my loose ideas of karma broke down and became replaced by that of grace, a terrible concept if I think too hard about it—the idea that the worst and most undeserving of us might also receive love.

It was a busy Friday night as Friday nights go. I was my typical, bitchy self because change doesn't happen overnight, and I demanded orders from customers because I was also hungover. Halfway through my shift, a dark-haired, cheery young man stood a foot away from the bar and grinned at me.

Are you gonna order a fucking drink or what? I shouted at him.

The bouncer sauntered up next to the stranger. *What—you don't recognize your cab driver from last night?*

My walls crumbled. I sprinted out from behind the bar and gave the cheery young man the best hug I could muster. Then I gestured frantically toward the closet and babbled about needing to grab my purse and write him a hefty check to clean his car and replace his clothes. *Plus the cab fare.*

I owe you over sixty dollars in cab fare. How much do you want? Two hundred? Three hundred? I mean, I probably owe you for saving my life.

The taxi driver—true story—just laughed.

Don't worry about it, he said. *I just came by to make sure you're alright.*

Then he handed me a tangerine and walked out of the bar.

III.

It's here in all the pieces of my shame
that now I find myself again.

— Rainer Maria Rilke

Bipolar II Disorder: Second Evaluation
(Zuihitsu for Bianca)

We all called her Bianca. My fever, my havoc, my tilt. *Bianca trashed the kitchen. Bianca scratched the shit out of me. Bianca owes me a mattress, owes me money, owes me cigs.* It was funny sometimes. It was a joke.

/

Bianca would spin the car up and down the highway. Night after night, she'd steer while picturing her rickety red Kia, her silver Hyundai sliding down a track of ticker tape, unfurling, unfurling.

/

Psychiatrist: *You would drink upwards of ten alcoholic drinks a day, every single day, then the minute you decided to stop, you'd just stop?*   *That's not alcoholism.*

/

My brain, a wheel. The rim: Bianca up, itching to shred the asphalt. The center: Bianca down, fetal-curled. For years, I crawled—up, down—its spokes. One spoke was a river, but I couldn't swim. Another spoke, a live wire. Yet another was a man I climbed like a tree. If I am stretching the metaphor, he, too, I felled.

/

Bianca, age 24: Not a metaphor: I walked in on an angel smoking a pipe in the tub.

/

Bianca, 20: I keep conjuring my friend's mother, who's been dead since he was a child. I see her sitting on the planter outside Sproul Hall each night I leave the boy in his bed to slink back to mine.

/

I comb through my chaotic stockpile of journals and notes—ebullient ~~convictions~~ delusions about the Universe, its Magic. Glittery pronouncements about every ~~*Godincidence*~~ *coincidence* on numerous short-lived blogs taken down and archived *for doctoral students who will* ~~*surely study me.*~~

/

Bianca, 26: What I said: "I just got my period. That explains the last 72 hours." His reply: "The stock market crashed. Colossal. Today." And can you believe it took me more than a minute to assure myself the two weren't related?

/

Months after the miscarriage,   sertraline. The psychiatrist warned that for some people, antidepressants can, like the bullfighter's muleta, incite mania. *Let's do it,* I said. If ~~the bipolarity~~ Bianca is there, let her show her horns.

/

Bianca, 33, scales a pole made of silk. She tears through the city in a wig, ice blue. She sneaks shots of well whiskey on her way to the bathroom. She mistakes my husband for a pointillist painting, which alarms her. She mistakes my husband for a collage of every man who has ~~threatened to call~~ called the police *because you're acting fucking crazy,* which makes her scream. She screams at my husband who, like the others, is saying, *Please. We are only two blocks from home.*

/

The diagnostic experiment catapulted me into *a mixed state.* Bianca up, Bianca down, all at once. Imploding and exploding, all at once. Collapsing, expanding. The widening Universe squirming inside an expired star caving in on itself.

/

Bianca, 28: *That was by far the most dysfunctional trip back to California. My brain wants to erase it, so I will record it here. I trust I will find it years from now as an older, wiser self who will know how to process this. Hello. Are you here now? Have you solved my brain?*

/

For 33 years, I had no framework for my torment. Vocabulary—a powerful reshaping tool. An agent of grace. Before *Complex PTSD* made sense of the senseless, I blasphemed Bianca with the rest of them. *Crazy, overreacting, psychotic, irrational.* Like that time I blew through California and   . *But someone you loved had died. And it was Father's Day. And your mother had concealed her car accident, her totaled car, then said someone with powers healed her by touching her head so she didn't need to see a doctor.*

/

When Legion—the cave-dweller who slashed himself with stones—was freed of his demons, two thousand spirits flew from his body into a herd of pigs.

/

I am seeing my whole life the way one looks at an ancient painting restored to its original vibrancy. *The Last Supper,* revived after the fires. A miracle it survived the bombings that decimated the rest of the church.

/

Bianca, 29: *Which came first? Everything falling apart or the feeling of everything falling apart?*

/

Bianca, 22, Easter: *I hate the tedium of having to go to bed and having to wake again. Death, resurrection, every damn day. My life is miraculous. My life is shit. There is something that doesn't want me to be. There is something that wants me to be so much.*

/

Possessed, Legion's pigs charged into the lake and drowned. I have imagined this until it has made me sick. Bianca, flung from my body into a hoofed thing, shrieking as she sinks.

/

The highs, the plummets, all so ~~fucking~~ obvious now. My father, my aunt, my sister. How did no one notice? Why didn't anyone know anything about it? The genetics of it. Its relationship to environment. Why was there no one to warn us? To help us? To prevent us from smashing our lives to bits with it? *Why did we all leave her when it was her turn, when it was her brain cranking it up?* ~~*It wasn't your fault. You were on the opposite coast. You were trying to survive.*~~

/

Boyfriend to Bianca, 21: *I called, but you didn't answer. I called the apartment, and C said you weren't there, so I kept calling you, then C answered your phone and said they thought you were in the bathroom. They got the door open, and you were passed out inside. They called me, and I came over to check on you. Your pulse is fine, so no risk of alcohol poisoning. You're just really tired.*

/

Although N asked once. N who, next I heard,   had died by suicide. In response to one of my blog posts: *Has any medical professional ever told you they think you might be bipolar?* And a link to José James's cover of "Autumn in New York." An update about his wife.

/

And M, who said to Bianca, 20: *Imagine shaking a root beer bottle. You shake it up good. Then you open it carefully and close it really fast so it doesn't explode. And you do this over and over until it can open without the soda spilling over. Or you try to do this, but it still overflows. Or you just open it without thinking, and it pours out. You are that bottle of root beer.*

/

Bianca, 21: *The rain screams down. It screams and screams like a child pitched down the stairs so hard she splits her head open on a jagged corner like a summer melon gashed by a stake. Ask me again about the weather.*

/

I hear the diagnosis, but it's like I am watching someone else's christening. Bianca swathed in white and rolling her new name in her mouth like a Lemonhead. Too sweet. Bright but not bright enough.

/

Even with a miswired, misfiring brain, I did this. I accomplished this. Imagine what I could have done with your brain is a thought that has made ~~Bianca~~

me want to jump off the roof.

/

What is it like to sail through life with a brain as ordered as a map? My maps are printed backward. With cities missing. Cities mislabeled, cities discolored, cities scrambled to look like a pile of plastic alphabet magnets. Cities with *Bianca Bianca* scrawled all over like a hex. Cities zoomed in so outrageously sometimes I make out half a street name and still, I am expected to navigate.

/

Bianca, 25: *A cloud hangs around the sun like a noose. No monsters under the bed this morning. They must have already snaked into my brain.*

/

To save me from the sertraline, quetiapine. To pull me up, but not too up. My headphones, full volume, loop electronic dance music: *I want it to be so badly, I wanted to be so badly, what you see in me, what you see in me.*

/

And every now and then, a friend: *And I kept thinking, too bad Eugenia's not around, she would totally bring out Bianca and have her bitch-slap him for me. Then I missed your face.*

Off the Medication: New Year's Eve 2019

I am raving
in this rain, this cloak
of coarse diamonds. Each drop
a door to the years that knocked me
dead. I am rich meat
in this rain. Insufferable. Crushed ice
in my fists, I am
parched. I beg Moses to call off
the plague of frogs

and when Moses asks when,
I am Pharaoh saying, *Tomorrow.*
God, I love the frogs.
God, make the plague stop.
My baby motions for a song
about speckled frogs,
and when I count the creatures
down to zero,

I don't know how
to swim again, twenty-something
at the dawn of this decade, on a raft
slapping through the Nile where
I held on through the Bad Place

then shot out into a rapid called
the Other Place.

I am the names
they used to bind me.
Firecracker. Sore for sight eyes.
Worthless whore. Every word,
cogent in this storm.
Even the ones that wish me

dead. I am the biblical woman
who, bleeding, cleaves the crowd
to finger a fringe
as a way of asking for help.
I have trouble asking for help.

Everyone has trouble
asking what kind of bloody help
and I can't stop screaming
the song that makes the frogs

bolt into a pool and croak.
I've taught my baby to sign for *all done*
and *more.*

God, I am done.
God,

I want more.

Post-Traumatic Stress Disorder with Han (한/恨)

What possessed me
to try to break my husband's arm

when he took the baby from me,
when he wouldn't surrender the baby

even as—especially as—I, animal
brained, clawed his flesh, drawing

blood from four crescents as I bent
his arm behind him? The previous

night, my father had checkmated
my silence with a photo of him dying

of cancer. Pale and wrinkled
as winter silk, he glared at the callous

lens of his phone, which he angled
down like a topless teenager,

like he needed to prove his cancer
to me, who received the photo twice

in case the first didn't go through.
For seven years, I'd imagined

my father dead. Then he bubbled up
everywhere—his emails, dozens,

all at once—like the time
the apartment above us paused

its demolition for a storm,
and we woke to our ceilings and walls

puffed and cracked, our kitchen floor
sunken in from the weight of the leaks.

My husband is not the first man
I've attacked. Malignant carcinoma,

pleural effusion plus three to six
months to rework the ending. Jesus—

if author, then a slack perfecter—
straps a mask to his face, scrubs

his punctured hands of us.
I am more God than God is

these days. Watch me refuse
to let my father die

in this poem. He is dying, yes,
but see how I keep him flickering

with a gerund? My father's body
deflating. Dehydrated stalk. A selfie

for Christ's sake. Alone as the day
he was released like a scream

from the mouth of an American
prison then expelled like an object,

foreign, from the American body
to a country neither his nor mine

but home to the ghosts roiling
our blood. To be Korean

is to house rage. Palpable rage.
Our people, collectively unwilling

to let go, believe we share
a turbulence, *a complex emotional cluster*.

Hateful resentment. The urge
to tear off my husband's limb.

Our brains: paper mausoleums.
We spark, we scorch, combust. I, too,

want to believe my violence
isn't all mine. The last of my father's

faces I saw fourteen years ago, before
I fled from it like a battered wife

instead of like the thing
packed in the backseat as usual.

I did reply, but like a politician I said
I am praying for him. But I don't

pray like someone who believes
in miracles, so what's the point?

Did I say my father's father
was an orphan in the war? Did I say

he died of the same thing
killing my father now? Even when I

don't want everything to be connected—
threads everywhere. Our people know

this. The iron taste of war in the mouth
screaming, *Give me my fucking baby.*

Orpheus calming the storm,
then Jesus calming the storm. Me

running from my father running from
his father running from the oppressor

back when we called them oppressors.
Did Orpheus sleep through the storm

the way Jesus slept through the storm?
On the cushion, Mark wrote. As if to say,

rested comfortably. Like someone
who didn't fear. Or didn't give a fuck.

Do you not care that we are perishing?
Every time I cried out

from my nightmares—my mother shot
in the face by my father at the door,

mother drowning in a purple lake,
mother plummeting from a cliff,

mother crushed three ways
by Cerberus—my mother laughed.

I can't die yet. I still have work to do here.
And because I believed her,

I get to grieve not only death,
but also the idea of death

as a reasonable creature who waits for
the neat finales of our redemption arcs.

Shy of sixty, my father says
he hasn't even begun the work

he set out to do. Even my foolishness
burns like rage. The shedding

of my childhood myths—rage.
The letters I folded exactly one way

and stuffed into envelopes—
boxes of them—for strangers

who, I prayed, would embrace my father's
newest hustle. The vending machines

my mother bought then couldn't sell.
The packs of cactus pills I order now

for my father who insists cactus pills
might kill the cancer. Who wouldn't

indulge a dying man's mania?
Who wouldn't let him believe

his delusions about the life he will live
once the cancer, advanced as it is,

vanishes? So I send what I can,
short of myself. The pandemic

dissuades the impulse flight anyway.
Still, my father begs for a reaction.

The kind a daughter might give.
But I am terrified

of the part of my brain that registers
my father in front of me and not

someone I don't want to hurt.
So I am impassive. Unreachable.

I am pawing the ocean floor
for blue holes the paper promised—

tunnels too small for submersibles
but wide enough for divers

to swim through to find a sanctuary
of glassy water ornamented

with tremendous displays of plants,
kingdoms of unexpected fish.

Please. I need to believe
all this plunging into the past

will yield an oasis like this. Tell me
when I hit the bottom of this ocean,

I will wind up not dead,
but through.

Now Show Me Your Glory

We harm
our stunning bodies. We repent

every time. Forever climbing out
from our mud into your mess

of feathers and music, everything
ringing of angels,

we reek of borrowed lovers.
Welcome us at your will.

But if you ask us to praise you
beneath your minced stars

and sky flat with artifice,
show your blistering face.

Pry open our mouths. Force
worship to rumble from our lips

like crows   flung
from a quaking wire.

The Mechanics of Survival

I smoked my first cigarette next to a trashcan
spray-painted *W-R-S-H-P*—

a call to worship in the bowels
of Will Rogers State Historic Park.

I sucked down my last
the day a Boeing 737 dove into the sea outside Bali,

and all one hundred and eight passengers
survived. Let's tell more stories

like this one. About the time buildings yielded
to the earth on my right,

while the ocean soared scraper-high on my left.
The planet in seizures,

I begged pardon for the years I'd wished to die,
and gunned it like the Israelites

wild across the split sea.
My husband materialized next to me.

Then twelve of us. Forty more. And in the end,
nine billion, hand in hand,

charged from our erupting world.
I woke next to the yellow note taped to my wall—

a handwritten list of the people I love
and the mountains they've slipped from.

Each morning, I touch their names.
I picture the friend, the sister, then picture the sun

pulling for us between wreckage and waves—
a hand in a crevice feeling for its lost ring.

Reionization

About 13.8 billion years ago, just 400,000 years or so after the big bang,
the universe abruptly went dark.... Eventually this fog would lift,
but how it did so is a question that has long baffled astronomers.

— *Scientific American*, Volume 310, Issue 4, April 2014

Not long after the big bang—
   God's first holy call and response—
     the universe went dark.

    All that hot bliss of brilliance
  shut inside a tomb. God
second-guessing

both *Let there be* and *light*.
   We know how the power went out:
     the cosmos cooled, then birthed

    hydrogen, which swallowed the glow.
  The name for that switching off of spark:
recombination.   Depression. Grief.

But we don't yet know

how the power returned.
      One theory imagines the first stars

        banded together, and their tenacious light
    knifed the dark apart: reionization.
Resurrection.   It's possible, then,

if we believe our astronomers and angels,
    that our abyss is temporary—
      that a young soprano of stars

        gathers now on the other side
        to sing the crucified to life.

The Commitment to Living Contract

On my bed, Dr. Kate's high-definition head rests
on an unopened box of panic-stashed paper towels. Beneath

the boxspring: a stack of art my husband and I have racked up.
Four years in this home I've known longer than every other

home, yet I haven't put up a single frame.
Maybe a fallout of childhood, of being forced to abandon

all my things those nights I was dragged from bed
to the next dump or safehouse before my father

returned. Our favorite from the pile: a twenty-inch print
of Tom Fruin's *Watertower*, the patchworked

Plexiglas monument whose sun-pierced pinks, reds, salt whites,
and ceruleans mute even our worst fights on the BQE

as we point to the sculpture in silence—a ritual—
whenever we drive by.   *I will ask you this directly.*

According to the web, a waxing gibbous moon looms
lucid above my drape-shut dot in Brooklyn. I survey

Dr. Kate's cabin walls, her generous rows of windows
all undressed, and through them, a Colorado gloaming so soft

I could wrap myself in it.   *Are you having thoughts of suicide?*
I have not made plans to die. *Are you—*

I am too afraid of drowning to consider, seriously,
the bridge.   *Are you having thoughts of suicide?*

If a tanker were to hit me, it wouldn't be the worst thing.
Suicidal ideations.   But I stop at the stoplight.

The naked white bedroom wall I square my back into
humiliates me. I was rarely allowed outside as a child.

The upside: I found it familiar, painless, to shelter in place
for sixty-eight days in this unpainted 950-square-foot box.

Do you remember your safety plan? You last signed it three years ago.
We revisit it. Revise it. Reload it. Restock it. We examine

my reasons for dying. For living. We *review, summarize,*
and highlight my *ambivalence* about *suicide.*

Risk factors. *How did you try   those times you tried?*
And protective factors. She tells my husband, my gentle,

genial husband, to hide the pills. Any pills, all the pills.
I will waffle between impressed and shredded

when I find, weeks later, that he hid them after all.
Then the *strategies.* Ways to assuage pain:

Tip your body chemistry (grab an ice cube).
Distract from emotional triggers (binge-watch a crafting competition).

Self-soothe your five senses (play the call of a cardinal,
smell bacon, taste bacon, chuck cheap eggs in the tub, *make*

one corner of the room beautiful). Improve the moment
(treat my toddler to a campy reading of *Bee-Bim Bop!*).

Resist the urge to pop this, smoke this, brew this, snort this,
sip, swig, or shoot this away. Then the list of names,

numbers. The last of whom is my husband. Then the hospital.
I taught my one-year-old to count to one hundred

before he could say his own name right. It's possible
I did this to hear him chant the only address he's ever known.

We leave home five minutes early for everything
to give him time to admire the 42 out front. For weeks

he pushed every 4 he could find next to every 2
before I remembered *The Hitchhiker's* answer

to *the Ultimate Question of Life, the Universe and Everything: 42.*
Do you agree that one of your counseling goals is to live a long life

with more pleasure and less unhappiness than you now have?
I agree. A life long as the deep-sea siphonophore. More

pleasure, yes, a colony of pleasure upon pleasure strung
together until I am the bioluminescent stinger, not the krill.

Do you understand that harming yourself or harming others is contrary
to achieving this goal?   Yes. I do understand.

How the Dung Beetle Finds Its Way Home

The Milky Way's glinting ribbon helps the dung beetle
roll his good ball of shit back to the ones he loves.
But blind him to the sky with as little as a hat,
and he will swerve like a drunk who, if he makes it home alive,

might find the family, soured with waiting,
gone. Drawers cleared, beds cold, even the watercolor ark
of giraffes and raptors pulled from the face of the fridge.
See? I want to tell my missing father, it's a metaphor so simple

it's almost not worth writing down: even beetles need the stars
to nudge them back to where they need to be
when they need to be there—toward their little ones'
gummy grins ever pardoning the grisliest parent.

I am thirty-four with a son the day my mother tells me
she enrolled in a four-day seminar about how to be a good mom.
A little late, I know.
Once, in a rage, I left my husband and our sleeping child.

Where did you go, friends ask when I tell the story.
I wish I'd had a grander plan. I wish I'd stood on the roof
of our building and, empowered by that single Brooklyn star,
I'd ripped up the book of my parents' sins.

Or I wish I could tell someone the truth: that I fear
I am the kind of woman who could leave the one good family
God had the gall to give her. Really,
I sat on the stairwell leading up to the roof and wept

until a large bug threatened my life, at which point I recalled
the dung beetles, stopped blaming my parents, and—
thanking the metaphorical stars—I rolled up my pile of shit
and trudged back home.

One Year after My Dying Father and I Stop Speaking to Each Other Again

Someone on the internet is mourning
her dad—*that old goat*—with a goldmine

of anecdotes. Scraps of fondness I scrape off
her tweet—his beef wellington, her frogs. I want

my frown-scored mouth loaded with her clean vocabulary
of love. The way she holds her father's hand, no pinch

of humiliation. Like the time I saw a teenager
sitting on her father's lap. How I couldn't

take my eyes off the alarming purity of it.
How my mouth dried at the sight like I had been drinking

the wrong water all this time. When I pull
the ocherous leaves from my thirsty pothos, it is

too easy. No satisfactory rip. Too ready
to let go. I covet the reels of the lucky ones going on

about their dead. Everyone I have lost
I have lost before the end.

The Cruelty

I expected to die much younger than I am now. Sometimes I think
I've already lived to the end of my life. And the life I live now
is the extra life. A complimentary mignardise. A delayed post-credits scene.
All of it, year after year, one quick clip. Unlike the punishing life
I stomached before this one. Those first three decades when the days
distended like years. The years, hideous millennia. The cruelty
of cruelty—the way one fetid second of suffering swells, expanding
like the universe. And crueler still, the years I've tasted since—

the one warm home in them, the love with whom I populated our nest
with my own fed body, those small pajamaed feet padding about
these gleaming floors, every quiet and colossal joy, year after year
of apple bread and bedtime songs and opulent peonies in June,
even Christmases that look and smell like Christmas—gone
like one damn day.

To the Self Who, Twelve Years Ago, Wrote a Letter to Me

Soon you'll drive from ocean to ocean to reboot yourself. And see
how deft you are at saving your life: here I am

nesting on the other side. You write to me from your nineteenth flight
in a manic year. All Cuervo and moxie. No address. You'd rather die,

you say, than wind up like me, serving the best scoops of my prime
to a man who chooses vanilla. You wouldn't like my desk,

two feet wide and screwed to a wall, or this blue crib monitor
ticking like a bomb waiting for the baby to go off. Your fears still

crackle in the corners of my better brain, a brain I've learned to water
and give access to sunlight. I remember the racket of plates

hurled in those homes that were not homes, and I hate
how I still hammer everything good until it matches the ugly warp

of my wounds. I hold my husband like I am afraid
I will detonate him. Like you, I know love is not a thing to be earned.

Only given, only lost. Like you, I forget this. We are not anyone
anyone wanted, but we were born anyway. Don't forget this.

After my wedding, I wept like a gwishin—like a white-gowned,
wire-haired ghost from a Korean horror story—for two blurred years.

I thought I'd fooled him into marrying me. A month before
he proposed, his entire family, including the children, gathered around

a cake with my name on it and sang a song with my name in it
to celebrate the fact of my birth. I couldn't take it—how easy it was

for them to be a family. Love should be more mysterious than this.
How else can I explain the decades lived without it? I've seen you

pray to a god you don't believe in. It's alright.
Your mouth is not the wrong mouth to ask for this. You question

who would take your body, who would take your blood.
Eat, drink, in remembrance of you. Let us keep the feast.

Bipolar II Disorder: Third Evaluation
(Ode to the Brain)

I am trying to cherish
this terrible city, this glittering city.

Oh, how its residents dance!
The basal ganglia

whiskey-whooping its luminous messages.
The tilted cerebellum

kicking offbeat. And the lobes—
all my disorder-

ly lobes—lush
and tuxxed, bopping in a line

not quite a line,
shaking their sparklers to receive me.

My Magic 8-Ball brain
spins with twenty answers for everything—all twenty,

yes. Yes, god-orb. Yes, sunstone.
Yes, synth-pop skull

fritzing with pop rocks. Yes, clock
miswound, clock on coals, clock

shotput to Elysium
and speeding with light. Tonight, I will not curse

the jagged slivers
you, crushed ornament, have

scattered everywhere.
I've neglected you for far too long,

you too-sweet fruit bruising in one blue spot, but—yes—
still good.

My Whole Life I Was Trained to Deny Myself

to please my father who'd make me
tiptoe from wall to wall then back again

to improve my lacking calves
or worm the ground like a vacuum

palming the carpet for bits of trash
he'd count in my little hands. When I spilled

a cupful of crushed chili flakes
on my Chapagetti noodles, he forced

the whole hot bowl down my throat
as I sobbed. And he ordered my hair pulled

back, always, in a ponytail. It wasn't until
I neared forty that I discovered

them—the women I'd twisted myself into
for the men I loved—all slumped in my gut

like a heap of secondhand costumes.
Once, I followed a man into a hurricane

minutes before it stripped half of Manhattan
from power. I trailed behind him

when the transformer line exploded
and the night sky flashed a ghastly

green like God smothering the city
with a neon sheet. Then the traffic lights,

streetlights, and every last lamp through
every window flickered then snapped,

and in that alarming darkness, the city shrank
into a closet so cramped I couldn't breathe.

Still, I stood in that downpour
on a sixth-story roof to hold up his boom mic

as he recorded the storm. For another,
I became a Ron Paul for President

groupie. I scanned Reddit in my homemade
campaign shirt while smoking weed

to white boy emo tracks about tommy guns
and existentialism the same year

I voted for Obama. For yet another,
I learned to ride a bike. Even managed one

from the Village to the GW Bridge,
but when the path clogged

halfway up with bikers on three sides of me
close enough to kiss, I forgot

how to brake. I threw out my hands
to grab the highway divider and collapsed,

then I hauled up the rental to finish the trek,
bloody knuckles and knees be damned.

And for hundreds of mornings, I woke
each morning before the morning—

not even two hours after last call in the city—
to blend spinach and strawberries

with flaxseed meal and hemp seeds for a man
to take to work. And when one provoked

a drunk stranger then couldn't meet a deadline
with his battered head, I let him

turn me into a comic book android.
I wrote pages upon pages of a monologue

he fed to the robot, fashioned
by a toymaker who loved her the way

he thought he loved me.
He injected her with scene after scene

from my childhood, and in the final issue,
haunted by my life, she screams,

Stop inventing me! before she claws open
her chest and yanks out a fat blue gem

carved like a heart. And during a spell
when I was shackled to no man, I got naked

in a room full of naked people, all of us
drunk and stoned, seated in a circle

like schoolchildren waiting for some game
to begin or for the morning hello song,

the kind that loops until you've hollered
everybody's name. At daylight, I drove

the prettiest of the girls home. The one
some men bragged they could bed

with a fat stack of C-notes, the one
who eventually married the mayor's son.

She had a habit of laughing
at everything everyone said and danced

with her hands above her head like someone
panicking with a pistol pointed at her face.

For years leading up to that day,
I thought she was the sort of woman

I was supposed to be—nonthreatening
with a body that inspired valuation.

She insisted she ride with me
instead of with the boys hovering over her

like a flight of hungry kestrels. And minutes
into the drive, it became clear she wanted

something from me, something like
absolution. Approval maybe.

And she said, *I feel sad.* And she said,
I don't know who that was, I don't know why

I did that—that being what we'd all done
all throughout the night, and I admit

I was rankled by her conscience, clanging
louder than mine, which was bored

of my neglect by then and resigned
to watching my life lurch forward without it.

When my father wasn't sculpting
or smacking me, he said I was made

in the image of God. So God I became,
forging myself each time I found a man

to die for. I was the creator, the crucified,
the wildfire slamming against their chests.

I read what they read, and I drank
what they mixed. I bent the way they bent me

to do what they invented. And how I charmed
their brothers. How I disarmed

their mothers—the lemony dolmas,
the pink pork meatballs I rolled with them,

the dough I pinch-pulled then dunked
in anchovy broth. And when I married

the last man I loved, as the woman
I thought I was, I woke one night

like a jinn horrified to find herself
fixed in her final incarnation. I stopped

recognizing myself to such a degree
that some days I'd wake having forgotten—

really, I'd forget—we had an actual child.
I morphed into a serpent, a tempest.

I struck myself against our domestic walls
like a mad bat trapped in a coop.

And my husband—who from the beginning
looked at me like he understood

I was not his, like he was willing
to take what he could get

for as long as I'd let him have it—refused
to enter my war. How bereft I was

left with no enemies. How I brawled
on that battleground alone with myself,

punching at nothing until I conjured
my multitudes. I wish I could say

I freed myself somehow. That I'd pried
those shadow selves from me

with a hex, a needle, a healing quartz.
Or that like the cloak of Bartimaeus,

they dropped in the dust
when I stripped myself to sprint toward

the savior's voice. No. By then, I'd lost
that appetite for discarding myself.

I carried them, one by one,
like bride after bride across the threshold

and removed their boots. I drew baths
loaded with salts, cooked meals in butter.

I let each one sleep when she needed to sleep.
And in time, I thanked them.

I came to recognize their service.
And in time, they let me love them the way

a father or a mother ought to have loved them.
Them.

Yes, I suppose I do mean me.

Gold

I've become
the kind of creature who, on Sundays,
fills seven small boxes with a bevy of pills

to stick it out another week.
When will I be fixed enough
to hear my kid scream without tearing

my father's phantom hands off me?
How do demons, decades gone now,
still ravage me? Tell me

I am not the thing
my child will have to survive.
Tell me

the mob I inherited will not touch
my son. Yes, the cavalcade
of all that's tried to kill me

may forever raid my brain, but know
this: in my mother's first language,
the word for *fracture,* for *crack,*

is the same as the word for *gold*.
Every Thursday for twenty-one months
before my son was born,

a doctor trained me to put the gun down
and write.   I understand
I am one of the lucky ones.

My Husband Tells Me about a Man
Who Doesn't Kill Himself

We are trapped in traffic beneath the overpass,
and the man in his story trembles on the edge

of an overpass eight hundred miles west of here. Here,
I have not tried to die for some years now.

The point of his story is the call
someone makes to nearby truck drivers. Together,

they gather beneath the man to form a net of big rigs
and wait for as long as it takes for a person to reconsider

the impossibility of tomorrow. I've known
the mangled shape the mouth makes begging someone

not to die. Which is different from begging her to live.
My husband's mouth, I think, makes this shape now.

All my life I thought I was hard to love.

Notes

The epigraph opening section I is from Anne Sexton's poem, "Cigarettes and Whiskey and Wild, Wild Women," published posthumously in *45 Mercy Street* (Houghton Mifflin, 1976).

Much of the italicized language in "Bipolar II Disorder: First Evaluation" was pulled from the American Psychiatric Association's *Diagnostic and Statistical Manual of Mental Disorders (5th ed.)*, commonly referred to as the "DSM-5," published in 2013.

The italicized lines in "Post-Traumatic Stress Disorder with Rovelli's Theories of Time" can be found in *The Order of Time* by Italian theoretical physicist Carlo Rovelli and translated by Erica Segre and Simon Carnell (Riverhead Books, 2018).

The epigraph for section II is from the poem "I Believe in This World" by Korean poet Kim Yideum and translated by Ji yoon Lee, Don Mee Choi, and Johannes Göransson in *Cheer Up, Femme Fatale* (Action Books, 2016).

Section III's epigraph is from *The Book of Pilgrimage* (II, 2) from Austrian poet Rainer Maria Rilke's *The Book of Hours.* The version excerpted here was translated by Anita Barrows and Joanna Macy (Riverhead Books, 2005).

The lyrics found in "Bipolar II Disorder: Second Evaluation (Zuihitsu for Bianca)"—"*I want it to be so badly, I wanted to be so badly, what you see in me, what you see in me*"—are from the song "love, or the lack thereof" by Isaac Dunbar.

In "Post-Traumatic Stress Disorder with Han (한/恨)," the interpretation of the Korean sociocultural concept of "han" is an intentionally clumsy one fumbling in the hands of a third-generation Korean American speaker and should not be conflated with or mistaken for scholarly work about han, which is ever-evolving in the United States, in Korea, and elsewhere. The purpose of han's cameo in this piece is to draw attention to its similarities to PTSD as experienced by the poem's speaker.

The phrase *"complex emotional cluster,"* which appears in "Post-Traumatic Stress Disorder with Han (한/恨)," is from *Excursions in World Music, Seventh Edition* (Routledge, 2017) in *Musics of East Asia II: Korea* by Joshua D. Pilzer.

"On the cushion" and *"Do you not care that we are perishing?"* which also appear in "Post-Traumatic Stress Disorder with Han (한/恨)," can be found in the English Standard Version of the Gospel of Mark, chapter 4, verse 38.

In "The Commitment to Living Contract," the phrases *"The Hitchhiker's"* and *"the Ultimate Question of Life, the Universe and Everything"* refer to Douglas Adams's novel, *The Hitchhiker's Guide to the Galaxy* (Pan Books, 1979).

Most of the other italicized lines in "The Commitment to Living Contract" were lifted from the safety plan referred to in the poem.

Acknowledgments

Many thanks to the editors of the following publications in which these poems, sometimes in earlier versions, first appeared:

> *The Academy of American Poets' Poem-a-Day, The Adroit Journal, AngryAsianMan.com, Bennington Review, Crab Creek Review, Drunken Boat, The Massachusetts Review, The Nation, Pleiades, Ploughshares, Poetry, Poetry Northwest, Rattle, The Rumpus, Spillway, Split This Rock, Tahoma Literary Review, Washington Square Review, Waxwing, The Yale Review*

"What I Miss Most about Hell" was selected by Eduardo C. Corral for the *2017 Best of the Net Anthology*, edited by Darren C. Demaree (Sundress Publications, 2018). It was also anthologized in *The World I Leave You: Asian American Poets on Faith and Spirit*, edited by Leah Silvieus and Lee Herrick (Orison Books, 2020).

"Prayer with Strawberry Gelatin" and "Reionization" also appeared in *Orison Anthology, Vol. 3, 2018*, edited by Luke Hankins, Nathan Poole, and Karen Tucker (Orison Books, 2018).

"Post-Traumatic Stress Disorder with Han (한/恨)" and "My Whole Life I Was Trained to Deny Myself" received *Poetry*'s 2021 Bess Hokin Prize.

"Gold" was anthologized in *The Long Devotion: Poets Writing Motherhood*, edited by Nancy Reddy and Emily Pérez (University of Georgia Press, 2022).

Lines from "Gold" were excerpted in Stephanie Foo's *What My Bones Know: A Memoir of Healing from Complex Trauma* (Ballantine Books, 2022).

Endless thanks to the Four Way Books team for your support, thoughtfulness, and diligent care of this book. To Martha Rhodes, Ryan Murphy, Sally Ball, Bridget Bell, Hannah Matheson, and everyone else working tirelessly at Four Way Books, thank you truly.

I owe a debt of gratitude to Traci Brimhall, Christina Pugh, Alan Shapiro, and Luis Alberto Urrea, whose workshops helped me locate the voice and direction of many of the pieces in this book. Thank you also to Kundiman, The Fine Arts Work Center in Provincetown, The Frost Place, and Brian Watkins formerly at The Center for Faith and Work for providing opportunities that were important to developing this manuscript.

I must also express overdue appreciation for and honor the women poets and writers, my former teachers, whose guidance from many years ago—and especially whose insistence on truth-telling—planted seeds in me that have germinated only now through the making of this book: Laure-Anne Bosselaar, Pam Dyer, Joy Harjo, Cathy Park Hong, Marie Howe, Harryette Mullen, Karen E. Rowe. A special thanks also to Julie R. Enszer, who mentored me with great compassion when I needed a mentor most, and to Lawrence-Minh Bùi Davis and Gerald Maa at the *Asian American Literary Review* for connecting me with Julie when I did not know how to steward this gift.

I am also grateful for these writers whose encouragement and support fueled me in ways both big and small on the long, circuitous journey toward this book: Neil Aitken, Hossannah Asuncion, Shaindel Beers, Justin Bigos, Michelle Chan Brown, Mahogany L. Browne, Kara Candito, Sherri Caudell, Tina Chang, Cathy Linh Che, Karissa Chen, Kirsten Shu-ying Chen, Jennifer S. Cheng, Su Cho, Victoria Cho, Noah Arhm Choi, Lisa Fay Coutley, Jessica Cuello, Oliver de la Paz, Danielle DeTiberus, Todd Dillard, Linda Harris Dolan, Johanna C. Dominguez, Stevie Edwards, Tarfia Faizullah, Karen Fish, Stephanie Foo, Sarah Gambito, Joan Kwon Glass, Janlori Goldman, Timothy Gomez, Sarah Kain Gutowski, Shannon Elizabeth Hardwick, April Naoko Heck, Lisa Hiton, Amorak Huey, K. Iver, Safia Jama, Davita Joie, I.S. Jones, Janine Joseph, W. Todd Kaneko, Sophie Klahr, E.J. Koh, Jason Koo, Hyejung Kook, Keetje Kuipers, Peter LaBerge, Iris A. Law, Christine Hyung-Oak Lee, Karen An-hwei Lee, Joseph O. Legaspi, Kenji C. Liu, Amy Long, dawn lonsinger, Ruth Madievsky, Sally Wen Mao, Victoria Lynne McCoy, Tyler Mills, Kamilah Aisha Moon (remembered dearly), Tawanda Mulalu, John Murillo, Matthew Olzmann, Sebastián H. Páramo, Emily Pérez, Joy Priest, Lynne Procope, Nancy Reddy, Patrick Rosal, Zohra Saed, Emily Sernaker, Purvi Shah, Sejal Shah, Brenda Shaughnessy, Jess X. Snow, Laura Swearingen-Steadwell, Kate Sweeney, Caitlin Elizabeth Thomson, R.A. Villanueva, Jericho Vincent, Cat Wei, Keith S. Wilson, Jane Wong, Haolun Xu, and the countless others whose voices I needed to hear during our exchanges, however brief, whether fortuitous or kismet (especially if we connected over snarky Instagram memes that helped us laugh about our mental health).

Thank you also to Christine Choe, Jessica Huang, Gina Kang, and especially Karissa Chen—the friends who remained "on call" as you pushed me to prioritize both my work and my pursuit of mental wellness during the writing of this book. And to the many others who appear in these pages—if not literally, then in spirit—as friends, roommates, and loved ones who showed grace to "Bianca" those many years ago (especially Shannon Fernando, Rini George, the other "Penguins and Trees," and Michelle Thompson, through whom I found the cover photo for this book), thank you for your humanity even when I was unbearable.

I could not have written this book without my access to empathetic, well-informed mental health professionals—a privilege I didn't always have and one I don't take for granted. I am forever indebted to Dr. Kate, whose work and whose heart have taught me to commit to this lifelong journey of healing. Gratitude upon gratitude to the other therapists and psychiatrists who have led to breakthroughs in my mental health: Dr. Kim, Dr. Park, Missy, Peter, and Dr. T.

In 2019, the National Institute of Mental Health estimated that in the United States, nearly one in five adults lives with a mental illness. This is a pre-pandemic number. On December 7, 2021, the New York Times reported that "in the United States, emergency room visits for suicide attempts rose 51 percent for adolescent girls in early 2021 as compared with the same period in 2019" ("The Pandemic Worsened Young People's Mental Health Crisis," written by Matt Richtel).

With statistics like these, it's likely that you, dear reader, know and love someone with a mental illness. Many of us have witnessed firsthand that one person's mental health can affect that individual's entire community. It's clear that mental health is a public health issue, and the inhumane struggle to obtain and afford adequate mental health care is a dangerous problem both in the United States and around the globe that must continue to be highlighted and addressed. Sharing our stories and destigmatizing mental illness is one small step, and I thank you for reading this book, for taking this step with me.

Finally, to my sisters, brave and resilient women that you are, I am eternally grateful for you. And to my husband, thank you for the ways you have supported the making of this book, and thank you for your patience as I learn to trust "home."

This book is for my child, who teaches me daily how to love, how to live.

This book is also for you who have known what it's like to hate your own brain. I hope we learn to love our brains soon.

EUGINIA,

MY NAME IS EDWARD,
I WAS WORKING AS A
TAXI THANKSGIVING EVE.
I GOT A CALL TO THE BRASS
MONKEY & BROUGHT YOU
HOME. YOU PUKED IN MY
BACK SEAT, & OVER THE
MOST OF ME. I CANNOT
QUITE UNDERSTAND WHY
THERE WAS NO ONE TO CARE
FOR YOU ESPECIALLY ON
A NIGHT LIKE THIS. IF YOU
WISH TO CALL ME YOU MAY
(818) ███████████ CELL

Eugenia Leigh is a Korean American poet and the author of one previous collection of poetry, *Blood, Sparrows and Sparrows* (Four Way Books, 2014). Her poems and essays have appeared in numerous publications including *Guernica*, *The Massachusetts Review*, *The Nation*, *Ploughshares*, *Poetry*, and *The Rumpus*. Poems from *Bianca* were awarded *Poetry*'s Bess Hokin Prize and selected for the *Best of the Net Anthology*. A Kundiman fellow, Eugenia received her MFA from Sarah Lawrence College and serves as a poetry editor at *The Adroit Journal*.

Publication of this book was made possible by grants and donations. We are also grateful to those individuals who participated in our Build a Book Program. They are:

Anonymous (13), Robert Abrams, Michael Ansara, Kathy Aponick, Jean Ball, Sally Ball, Clayre Benzadón, Adrian Blevins, Laurel Blossom, adam bohannon, Betsy Bonner, Patricia Bottomley, Lee Briccetti, Joel Brouwer, Susan Buttenwieser, Anthony Cappo, Paul and Brandy Carlson, Mark Conway, Elinor Cramer, Dan and Karen Clarke, Kwame Dawes, Michael Anna de Armas, John Del Peschio, Brian Komei Dempster, Rosalynde Vas Dias, Patrick Donnelly, Lynn Emanuel, Blas Falconer, Jennifer Franklin, John Gallaher, Reginald Gibbons, Rebecca Kaiser Gibson, Dorothy Tapper Goldman, Julia Guez, Naomi Guttman and Jonathan Mead, Forrest Hamer, Luke Hankins, Yona Harvey, KT Herr, Karen Hildebrand, Carlie Hoffman, Glenna Horton, Thomas and Autumn Howard, Catherine Hoyser, Elizabeth Jackson, Linda Susan Jackson, Jessica Jacobs and Nickole Brown, Lee Jenkins, Elizabeth Kanell, Nancy Kassell, Maeve Kinkead, Victoria Korth, Brett Lauer and Gretchen Scott, Howard Levy, Owen Lewis and Susan Ennis, Margaree Little, Sara London and Dean Albarelli, Tariq Luthun, Myra Malkin, Louise Mathias, Victoria McCoy, Lupe Mendez, Michael and Nancy Murphy, Kimberly Nunes, Susan Okie and Walter Weiss, Cathy McArthur Palermo, Veronica Patterson, Jill Pearlman, Marcia and Chris Pelletiere, Sam Perkins, Susan Peters and Morgan Driscoll, Maya Pindyck, Megan Pinto, Kevin Prufer, Martha Rhodes, Paula Rhodes, Louise Riemer, Peter and Jill Schireson, Rob Schlegel, Yoana Setzer, Soraya Shalforoosh, Mary Slechta, Diane Souvaine, Barbara Spark, Catherine Stearns, Jacob Strautmann, Yerra Sugarman, Arthur Sze and Carol Moldaw, Marjorie and Lew Tesser, Dorothy Thomas, Rushi Vyas, Martha Webster and Robert Fuentes, Rachel Weintraub and Allston James, Abigail Wender, D. Wolff, and Monica Youn.